KEEPING UP WITH THE JONESES? THEY'RE BROKE, TOO!

Vincent C. Perry

Cover designed by Myndshift I Integrated Marketing & Ad Agency

Vincent C. Perry, CFP®

Visit my website at www.vincentcperry.com

Printed in the United States of America

First Printing: Aug 2022
Name of Company

ISBN-13 979-8-218-05260-7

CONTENTS

"Too many people spend money they haven't earned to buy things they don't want to impress people they don't like."

   --- *Will Rogers*

"As a man thinketh in his heart, so is he".

   --- *Proverbs 23: 7*

"Only when you see something the way it is, will you be able to handle it sensibly."

   --- *Sadhguru*

INTRODUCTION

Do you sometimes compare yourself to others?

Come on, admit it – who doesn't? It's human nature. We need a gauge with which to measure success. Oftentimes, we measure our level of success based on the *perceived* success of others we see. I use the word *perceived* because we often think a person is successful based upon their outward appearance and the material things they have. However, upon closer inspection, we may find that, what we once thought was success, is nothing more than a carefully orchestrated façade, a mirage -- basically smoke and mirrors.

Many of the people that we hold in such high regard because we think they have "arrived" are only living a fantasy lifestyle. This lifestyle is not sustainable for them, nor anyone else in their socioeconomic class. Many of these folks are living well above their means, i.e., spending too much and saving too little. The casual observer does not, could not, nor would ever know that their finances are nothing more than a fragile, untenable financial house of cards.

In "*The Psychology of Money: Timeless Lessons on Wealth, Greed, and Happiness.*" Morgan Housel writes, [1]"Someone driving a $100,000 car might be wealthy. But the only data point you have about their wealth is that they have $100,000 less than they did before they bought the car (or $100,000 more in debt.). That's *all* you know about them."

As consumers of goods and merchandise, we have to become acutely aware of this tendency to want what others have. More importantly, we must become aware of our actions because of this unwise tendency to covet. Then, and only then, can we start the process of healing while achieving financial and emotional dignity. This dignity will not be achieved by using others' perceived success as a measuring stick. It will only be achieved by accepting and then embracing our economic reality, whatever that reality may be.

While the title of this book is "Keeping up with the Joneses? They're BROKE too!", the word *BROKE* is not meant to be pejorative or disparaging in any way.

For some members of society, the word *BROKE* says more about one's state of mind and less about cash flow. Many of us make good money yet have very few tangible assets to show for it. For far too many of us, being "*BROKE*" is more about our thoughts around money and our spending habits and less about monthly income or asset level.

Think about a couple who earns $9,000 per month but spend $8,900 of it. Sure, they have a good income, but are spending almost all of it and probably are not saving or investing any of it. So, as far as I am concerned, these individuals are "BROKE" —not based solely on their cash flow, but their spending habits.

Alternatively, think of a recent college graduate who earns $3,500 per month and saves half of it. She may not be considered a top income earner, but, in my opinion, she is most certainly not broke.

Some time ago, I read a quote by author and satirist Will Rogers that helps illustrate the point. He says: "Too many people spend money they haven't earned to buy things they don't want to impress people they don't like." [2] Let those words sink in for a moment and consider how nonsensical that behavior is.

It is crucial that we understand that people generally inherit behavior patterns and attitudes about money early on from the people who raised them. These patterns can develop before we even fully grasp the concept of money. In light of that, how would you answer these questions?

What is your earliest recollection of money?
Did your parents argue about money a lot?

Was there a time when your family went without certain things because they could not afford them?

Was there abundance in your home?

Whether we are consciously aware of it or not, the answers to these questions helped to shape our habits and how we think about money today. Those early memories and our current habits tend to determine our current financial station in life more than educational attainment, race, gender, or any other factor. Therefore, some people get stuck at their parents' level of financial status—whatever level that might be.

Fortunately, these financial habits can be changed and even erased over time IF we know how. We need to understand that our financial habits, whether good or bad, begin AND end in the mind.

Habits, by definition, are learned and anything that is learned can be unlearned. Thus, any poor financial habit can be changed by reframing our thoughts and engaging in the systematic and intentional acts we will discuss throughout the book.

MEET THE JONESES

By all accounts, our fictional couple, Mr. and Mrs. Jones, are a happily married couple. They have three children and four grandchildren. They just celebrated their Silver Anniversary.

After 25 years of mostly wedded bliss, they have experienced all the highs and lows of marriage.

They have poured their hearts and souls into raising their children and are now thoroughly enjoying spoiling their grandchildren.

They take part in neighborhood events and attend church regularly.

They volunteer at the local food bank and, on most weekends, work in their garden.

They have remodeled the kitchen along with all three bathrooms and they have closed in their patio.

They take a fabulous vacation every year and the occasional quick weekend getaway.

They have two fancy late-model cars and are now looking at an RV for future road trips.

When it comes to attire, only the latest and greatest will do. Their motto is, "If it looks good, wear it!"

Combined, they have a relatively nice income. They have been on their jobs for over 20 years each and are looking forward to taking early retirement.

Right now, though, they are not sure what retirement would look like. Because of their debt burden, they aren't sure if they will even be able to retire.

From the outside looking in, this is an All-American, picture-perfect couple, a couple most people would envy. The only problem for the Joneses is they are "*BROKE.*"

Again, don't misunderstand the word broke. They can pay most of the bills on time but have little savings.

They have raided their 401(k) accounts more than they care to admit.

Most of their credit cards, which have double-digit interest rates, are maxed out.

They occasionally have overdraft and late fees plus they have recently taken out a second mortgage on the house.

Even with their great income, they are essentially living paycheck to paycheck. If one of them were to lose their job or even have a pay cut, financial ruin would be right around the corner.

They have never really been overly concerned about their finances. That is, until they were turned down for a loan on the RV. The bank told them their debt-to-income ratio was too high.

"Our debt to what," they asked.

The banker smiled and kindly replied, "You have too much debt relative to your income, so, unfortunately, we cannot approve your loan."

You see, the Joneses just *assumed* that, since they had a high income and paid most of their bills on time, the loan would not be a problem. Getting this response from the bank was undoubtedly a shock because they had always been able to buy anything they wanted. Of course, they couldn't afford half of the stuff they bought, but having access to easy credit always made it possible... until now.

Our fictional couple, The Joneses, could be your neighbors, church members, colleagues, or in-laws.

They could live in the east, west, north, or south.

They could live in suburban, urban, or rural America.

Their house could be small, medium, or a mansion.

They could be white, Black, Latinx, or Asian.

They could make a lot or a little.

They could be Christian, Muslim, Jewish, or Atheists.

You see, the Joneses could, quite literally, be any couple around you and you would never know they were in such a state.

The reason you wouldn't know is simple—the Joneses rarely talk to each other about money at all, let alone to those outside of the marriage. When you see them, everything looks fine. It looks better than fine.

The yard is well-manicured.

The house is immaculate, inside and out.

The cars are always clean and they always seem to be having so much fun!

In seeing that, how would one know that the couple who seems to have it all together—the idyllic lifestyle and the seemingly perfect marriage—be on the verge of bankruptcy? You couldn't know.

The Joneses themselves don't understand the gravity of their financial condition. In medical terms, the Joneses essentially have Stage 4 terminal cancer. They just have not been diagnosed yet and, just like cancer, their reckless spending habits have metastasized to now affect their entire financial existence.

In their minds, they have just been living their "best" life without regard to the consequences of their spendthrift lifestyle. Unfortunately, their "best" life has been a wanton disregard of 'Finance 101'—to live below your means or, put another way, to spend less than you make. The Jones' motto is to, "Spend what you make, and then some!"

It seems that a decent income and access to credit are all the Joneses need to keep the illusion of financial health and that is precisely what it is −an illusion. It is smoke-in mirrors, a carefully orchestrated ruse to make those on the outside believe that they have arrived and achieved some level of financial dignity. In reality, they are only one missed paycheck away from financial ruin. Yet, most of those around the Joneses find themselves emulating them.

They want to be like the Joneses.

They want the Jones' lifestyle, but what they are emulating, is merely a façade.

They are emulating what they see, which is a false narrative of success.

If they pulled back the curtain and found out what a shamble the Jones' finances were really in, the Joneses would suddenly not be ones to mimic but pity.

Now let's look at our next fictitious family and see if there's a difference.

MEET THE PETERS

Now, let me introduce you to fictitious clients "Mr. and Mrs. Peters." (Disclaimer: I do not have any clients with that last name; however, the description of their actions and spending behavior is indicative of actual clients.)

The Peters are in their mid-sixties. Mr. Peters recently retired after working in manufacturing for over 30 years. Ms. Peters was a homemaker but worked several part-time jobs to help support the family. During their working years, their joint income did not exceed $82,000 in any one calendar year; however, their net worth is well over $1,000,000.

Net worth is simply the value of everything you own minus the value of everything you owe or assets minus liabilities. Folks, the Peters' net worth is approximately 12 times their average annual income!

Net worth at this level for them signifies robust financial health. In medical terms, someone with this level of physical fitness would compete in and sometimes win marathons.

To determine if one's net worth signifies financial health or not, we have to compare their net worth with their annual income and age. A couple like the Peters have been working and saving for over 30 years.

At this stage of life, you would expect them to have a net worth between 5 and 7 times their annual income. You would expect a couple in their mid-twenties, just starting their career, however, to have a net worth between 2 to 3 times their annual income.

The rationale for the difference in what connotes a healthy net worth is straightforward. Our young couple probably still has student loan debt.

They may be just starting a family.

Their incomes are relatively low.

They may have just taken out a mortgage for their home and have not had the same amount of time to accumulate wealth as the Peters. Also, since financial assets are such a significant contributing factor to net worth, you would expect their net worth to be lower than a couple who has been saving for much longer.

Back to the Peters. As we mentioned, their net worth is over $1,000,000. A healthy net worth for a couple in their mid-sixties, earning around $80,000 per year, would be between $400,000 and $560,000. Again, we are just multiplying their income times 5 (on the low side), or by 7 (on the high end). The Peters' net worth far exceeds even the high-end number.

Why is this? The answer is simple. They live below their means.

If their average monthly take-home pay is $5,000, they will spend LESS than $5,000 for that month.

They do not compare their lifestyle to others.

They are not concerned with the type of vehicle their neighbors drive nor how many square feet their relatives' homes are.

They are only concerned with their economic reality; and what their monthly budget looks like.

A budget, in its simplest form, is how much income is coming into your home, versus how much is leaving.

The Peters don't lease. Instead, they take out low-interest loans for their vehicles.

They finance those loans for 3 or 4 years on the high end and pay them off before they are due.

They drive their vehicles until the wheels fall off and, when they finally do replace their vehicles, they don't buy brand-new ones. They buy cars that are two or three years old.

They understand that depreciation can reduce the value of a new vehicle by 10% or more the moment they drive it off the lot.

They use credit cards responsibly, only buying what they need and then paying the balance off each month.

They don't need 346 different cable channels. The basics will suffice.

To them, a $1,000 so-called 'Smartphone' is not a very smart purchase. "Why pay for 40 megapixels, when 12 takes great photos," they will ask.

The fabulous vacation is only taken once every five to ten years. Most years, it is just a quick get-away that they can drive to.

They don't buy things they can get for free, from books (think of the library) to checking accounts (credit unions).

They buy things out of season when they are cheaper, shopping for decorations after the holiday is over, back-to-school items in the winter, winter wear in the spring, and patio furniture in the fall.

When they receive a windfall, such as a raise, tax refund, or contest winnings, they don't go on a shopping spree. Instead, they pay down any debt, invest, or save for a rainy day.

They take advantage of the competition. They get several price quotes, including fees and benefits, and see who wants their business.

As far as the Peters are concerned, you don't get what you pay for; you get what you ask for. If something is expensive, they haggle and, not just on cars and TVs, but everything from credit card interest to doctor visits.

They check for coupons online, using sites such as Honey and Retail Me Not, and in print before buying anything. On the other hand, they certainly don't let a coupon, or any other deal, convince them to buy something they weren't going to buy anyway.

Before they buy something new, they sell something old, which helps them offset the cost and creates more space.

They are not afraid of generics, especially when it comes to prescription drugs. They understand full well that generic drugs can be just as effective as brand-name, but at a fraction of the cost.

They don't pay for expensive extended warranties. Instead, they keep their items well-maintained and put the money they would have spent on the extended warranty in a savings account. That way, when/if something fails, they have a smart way to pay for it.

The Peters have no interest in keeping up with the Joneses or anyone else for that matter. They are only concerned with what happens under their roof.

They completely understand and live by one of my favorite phrases, "It's not what you earn – it's what you keep," and they plan to do everything they can to keep more of what they earn.

Most people aspire to be the Peters after they reach a certain age in life.

Why?

The next chapter will explain it.

WHY WE COVET

Exodus 20:17 says: "You must not covet your neighbor's house or anything else that belongs to your neighbor."

Merriam-Webster defines the word covet this way: "to desire (what belongs to another) inordinately or culpably."

The most important part of that definition is "what belongs to another."

You may want an all-wheel Suburban because it supplies a certain degree of safety and traction on slick roads to protect your family. Making that purchase for those reasons is practical, prudent, and makes perfect sense.

On the other hand, when we want that same SUV simply because a colleague or family member just bought one, this is when we start to covet.

The problem is not so much the desire to have what others have. The real problem arises when we act on that desire and walk into the dealership looking for that vehicle. To make matters exponentially worse, this is a vehicle that we don't need, may not want, and cannot even afford!

We need to understand the root cause of why so many of us compare ourselves to others in the first place and, more importantly, why we adjust and sometimes alter our lifestyle because of this comparison. This should come as no surprise, but we live in a capitalist society.

According to Investopedia, "a capitalist society is a social order in which private property rights and the free market serve as the basis of trade, distribution of goods, and development."

Capitalism essentially separates society into two classes of people: the Proletariat and the Bourgeoisie, or the "Haves" and the "Have-nots."

Capitalist societies tend to hold those with immense wealth, the "Haves," in high regard.

They are placed on a pedestal.

They are to be admired, envied, and emulated.

They are the best and brightest in society, regardless of their educational achievement. Invariably, those without wealth, the "have-nots,' can become envious and want what the "haves" have -- stuff!

To better illustrate the point, let's examine "Maslow's Hierarchy of Needs." According to Wikipedia, Maslow's Hierarchy of Needs is an idea in psychology proposed by Abraham Maslow. "It is used to study how humans intrinsically partake in behavioral motivation. Maslow used the terms "physiological," "safety," "belonging and love," "social needs" or "esteem," and "self-actualization" to describe the pattern through which human motivations generally move."

Let's further examine the fourth stage from Maslow's Hierarchy, "Esteem needs." Wikipedia defines this stage this way, "Most people have a need for a stable esteem, meaning which is soundly based on real capacity or achievement. Maslow noted a "lower" version of esteem is the need for respect from others and may include a need for status, recognition, fame, prestige, and attention."

Notice that Dr. Maslow did not call his theory the Hierarchy of *Wants*. No, he called it the Hierarchy of **Needs**. This esteem need can lead those without wealth to derive self-worth, or even self-esteem, from how they think society perceives them, not from morals or deeply held beliefs and values.

They want, maybe even need, to be liked, to be admired just like the Haves are appreciated and admired. Unfortunately, those of us who are without often try to garner this undue admiration not by degrees or titles but by "conspicuous consumption."

Conspicuous consumption is all about buying stuff, or material possessions, for the express purpose of being seen with said stuff. We're talking about handbags, shoes, clothes, cars, toys, big, fancy toys. This is not just run-of-the-mill stuff, but name brand, big-ticket, expensive stuff.

The acquisition of these things tends to make us feel good about ourselves.

It makes us feel special.

It makes us think we have arrived.

It makes us feel like we belong.

We may not have immense wealth, like the Haves, but we are now to be admired and looked up to.

But why?

Why are we to be looked up to suddenly? Is it because we were to able charge a pair of overpriced Gucci's on a maxed-out credit card?

That's nonsense and also financially destructive.

We sit back and watch when others in our orbit buy things. If we are not careful, though, we can become jealous, either consciously or unconsciously. Suddenly, we are not as special as we were before.

Our self-esteem somehow is tarnished.

Our perceived status is diminished.

We have suddenly become less than—less than the ones who increased their debt load by buying unneeded material possessions.

How nonsensical is that?

This phenomenon is especially true as it relates to those closest to us, those in our orbit, particularly with those who, for some unknown reason, we seem to think are successful.

We have to outdo Cousin Bob or the folks across the street, so we go out and buy a brand-new car like Bob did. We do not buy just any car—oh no! We buy a car that's nicer, of course, than the one Bob bought.

The problem is that neither one of us can afford that new ride, but who cares because it makes us feel good, right?

We buy it despite the financial consequences.

Who doesn't enjoy the green envy we stir up in others when they see us pull up in that brand-spanking-new ride or when we post the pictures on Facebook or Instagram of that fabulous vacation we just took?

Does this not make us feel better about ourselves?

Sometimes just wanting stuff or truly needing stuff is immaterial. The urge to 'one-up' our co-worker supersedes rational thought. To discover how irrational the Joneses' behavior can be, one needs to look no further than their closet.

Their closet is jammed-packed with garments and shoes that have barely been worn. You can even find the price tag still on some items, yet you can still find Mr. or

Mrs. Jones in line at the local department store with some of those same items in hand.

The truth is no one is immune from this tendency to over shop. One day my wife and I were looking to put away some things we recently purchased. The problem was that every single closet in the house had stuff in it. There were winter clothes, summer clothes, shoes, boots, and coats, you name it! Each closet had some of these items inside. It was sad and a real revelation for us.

If left unchecked, this type of behavior can become destructive. Reckless, wanton spending has sent way too many Americans straight to Bankruptcy court, Divorce court, and if still left unchecked, criminal court.

The problem with this behavior is that it can devolve into an illness I like to call "Spenditis." One minute, you are basking in the joy you feel from your brother-in-law's green with envy stare. The next thing you know, you're being served with an eviction notice.

Spenditis is not a "one-off" where one makes an impulsive purchase, and that's it. No! Spenditis is a pattern, behavior, and habit where one buys, buys, and buys some more.

They buy until the credit cards are maxed out.

They buy until each closet in the home is full and, just like hypertension, diabetes, or many other illnesses,

Spenditis can sneak up on you before you even know what hit you.

Piling up mounds and mounds of debt does not happen overnight. We see this same insidious trend with an obese person. It happens slowly, day after day, week after week. The result looks dramatically and surprisingly different from the starting point.

We keep spending because we can because we have access to credit. This credit; however, is like water from a well. It's refreshing while it lasts but, at some point, it runs dry and, unfortunately, for those poor inflicted victims of Spenditis, there is no flashing red light signaling danger ahead.

There is no one telling us to stop this irresponsible behavior or, if someone is telling us to stop, we don't listen.

I mean, we're adults.

You work hard for your money.

You deserve to have nice things and no one can tell you otherwise.

The question should not be if you deserve nice things, but what are these nice things costing you. The cost I'm referring to is not what's on the price tag. That is easy to quantify, but to the toll it takes on your finances, your emotional well-being, and, most importantly, your family. That cost is immeasurable and the effect is long-lasting. It all boils down to getting our priorities straight.

Nice things are, well, nice and it's true that, when you work hard, you should be able to treat yourself to nice things from time to time. The thing to keep in mind is that these nice-to-haves should not and cannot come at the expense of have-to-haves.

We all know the difference between nice-to-haves and have-to-haves. The have-to haves are the basics: food, water, clothing, and shelter. Nice-to-haves are everything else. We need to stop for a moment and closely examine have-to-haves. For example, we all have to eat, but we don't always have to eat out.

Have you ever looked at your cable, phone, or internet bill? Chances are excellent that you are paying more than you need to for those services. Most service providers have some sort of customer retention department. That department's sole purpose is to keep you as a customer.

Ask to be transferred to that department and you will be surprised how they can 'magically' reduce the amount you are currently paying without changing any of your existing services. This is all about keeping more of your hard-earned dollars in your pocket and less of it in theirs.

Another example would be clothing. In today's "polite society," you would be wise to wear clothing while out and about, but does all your clothing need to be made by Gucci, Louis Vuitton, or Prada? I would respectfully suggest that it does not.

You are paying a hefty premium for the permission to wear that fancy logo on your handbag.

Think about it.

Are those shoes worth three times as much just because the soles are painted red?

Is that cup of coffee at Starbucks worth four times one you can easily make at home?

I think not.

We cannot allow our self-worth to be driven by the acquisition of things. Things that have no intrinsic value depreciate. Things only bring temporary joy. The joy that is driven by the "Law of Diminishing Marginal Return."

According to Investopedia, "The law of diminishing marginal returns is a theory in economics that predicts that after some optimal level of capacity is reached, adding a factor of production will result in smaller increases in output." Or, for our purposes, smaller increases in satisfaction.

To illustrate this theory, let's examine a story based on the first and most important of Maslow's Hierarchy of Needs, Physiological Needs.

Imagine a husband, a wife, and their two children being lost in the woods with no shelter of any kind. They are cold, hungry, and afraid. Suddenly, they come upon a one-room shack that has a wood-burning stove. That lowly, meager structure supplies just the basics for survival: warmth, a degree of safety, and a place to lay their heads at night.

Compared to the danger and cold of the woods that they were used to, the basics offer an unbelievable amount of satisfaction for this family. They are warm. They are safe and can finally get a good night's sleep.

After living in the shack for a while, the young family makes their way out of the woods and can rent a two-bedroom apartment. The apartment, while small, has a bathroom and a kitchen. They are elated. The apartment also supplies some nice amenities that are helpful, and it is larger than the shack.

Soon, a new addition to the family comes along. The apartment has suddenly become a bit cramped.

They now need a larger space.

They have saved and can finally buy a three-bedroom house.

The kids now have a backyard to play in.

Mom and Dad have their own space as well.

The house supplies happiness and joy, but not as much pleasure as either the apartment or the shack provided. They are content in their three-bedroom home.

One day, they decide to buy a ticket for a charity event to win a dream home. As luck would have it, they win! This is a beautiful, spacious, 5,000-square-foot house with every feature imaginable.

The family takes a tour of their fabulous new home. They have never seen a house this big. The parents ask the kids if they like it.

The kids reply, "Yeah, it's okay." The husband asks the wife if she likes it.

She replies, "It sure is big. Someone has to clean this big house." The wife asks the husband what he thinks.

He replies, "That's a mighty big yard I'll have to cut." Well, wait a minute now! Just two years ago, this family was homeless, cold, and frightened out in the woods. Now, they have been blessed with a 5,000-square-foot mini-mansion and no one is all that excited.

How could that be?

With each successive move, their enthusiasm diminishes a bit, so the house that some would consider a fabulous dream home is received as just another shelter for them. Put another way, if the family had received the mini mansion as opposed to the shack when they were cold and afraid in the woods; they would have experienced the same joy and elation at that moment. That is because their basic needs would have been met by both structures. But with each successive move, the joy diminishes a bit.

Sometimes we yearn for a mansion because we think it will bring us infinite joy, respect, and admiration from others when a clean, comfortable home with a backyard and a fence will do fine and is probably much more affordable.

More is not always better. Sometimes, more is just more, but we may not be able to see this when we are trying to gain an advantage over our so-called friends and relatives.

The Peters fully understand this theory and know that bigger is not always better. Sometimes, bigger is just bigger.

They are quite content with having enough.

Enough food to eat.

Enough shoes and clothes.

Enough square feet in their home.

Enough stuff.

They don't need more, more, more.

They just need...enough.

WHY I WROTE THE BOOK

The "Great Recession" of 2008 was the greatest economic downturn in the United States since the Great Depression of the 1930s. As a result of the Great Recession, the United States alone shed more than 8.7 million jobs. According to the U.S. Bureau of Labor Statistics, this caused the unemployment rate to double. According to the U.S Department of the Treasury, American households lost almost $19 trillion of net worth because of the stock market plunge.

Large, medium and small businesses alike were affected. Some businesses lost significant revenue. Others simply closed for good. My financial planning practice certainly was not immune.

Early in 2008, I hired a new administrative assistant and increased the size of my office space, doubling the amount of rent I was paying. As a result of the stock market crash, most clients wanted nothing to do with investing more assets in anything even though that might have been a prudent, sound strategy for them.

With the value of their existing assets depreciating every week, convincing them to invest more of their hard-earned dollars during a stock-market freefall was a tall order. You really could not blame them - fear was running rampant.

I was hit with an economic one-two punch. My monthly expenses increased just as my revenue dramatically decreased.

I was supplying financial advice to others during my economic crisis! The crisis I was in was not one brought on by what most would consider irresponsible actions on my part.

I was still in the same precarious situation as those who may have made imprudent financial decisions.

I could relate and empathize with them.

I felt their pain.

I had a taste of the fear they were experiencing, and I didn't like it.

The Coronavirus pandemic of 2020 wreaked havoc on the economy, killing or sickening millions of Americans. Many businesses were forced to shut down temporarily, and some closed for good. The businesses that did survive had to lay off employees just to keep the doors open.

As a result, the pandemic laid bare those who previously either spent too much or saved too little. In an article published by CNBC, it is estimated that over half of Americans have $5,000 or less in savings.

25% of survey respondents indicate having no emergency savings at all, up from 21% who said they didn't have any in 2020.

Another 26% say they have some emergency savings, but not enough to cover expenses for three months. [3] This was happening in the greatest and richest country on earth? These statistics are staggering! Unfortunately, this is the sad reality for far too many Americans and it is completely unacceptable.

As a Certified Financial Planner Professional (CFP®), I have come across many individuals during my over two decades in the financial advice industry.

These individuals run the gamut.

They are young and old, black and white, rich and poor.

Some are politically progressive or conservative.

They live on the east coast, the west coast, the north, and the south.

Some are aggressive investors while others are risk averse.

Some are frugal, and some are spendthrifts.

These last two characteristics tell you more about their ability to achieve financial dignity than either of the former combined.

My motto is simple: 'It's not what you earn – it's what you keep.'

It matters little what you look like, your station in life, or your present financial circumstances. What matters most is how you treat the financial resources that you have been blessed with.

You could earn $40,000,000 per year, or $4,000. If you are not saving and investing some of it, it matters not.

You might say, "How could someone earning $40,000,000 per year not be saving or investing, let alone go broke?"

To answer that question, we only need to look at a few individuals who have done just that. In an article published by Business Insider[4], they list names such as Nicolas Cage, Mike Tyson, 50 Cent, MC Hammer, Kim Basinger, Burt Reynolds, Willie Nelson, and Larry King. Even the King of Pop himself, the great Michael Jackson was reportedly at least $400 million in debt when he died unexpectedly in 2009.

To further illustrate the point, statistics show that 70% of lottery winners end up with very little of their winnings, and according to the National Endowment for

Financial Education, a third go on to declare bankruptcy.[5]

It is important to remember that, if one has poor spending habits before receiving sudden money, they will have poor spending habits after sudden money.

As I have mentioned several times so far, the term *broke* has nothing to do with income or asset level. It is all about your thoughts about money, and your spending habits. The one thing each of the individuals had in common is that they all suffered from the ailment discussed in the last chapter called Spenditis.

Unfortunately, I have seen far too many people sitting in front of me suffering from this ailment.

It is uncovered quickly from a cursory look at one's balance sheet, assuming they have one.

It can also be uncovered from a brief discussion of their age, income, assets, and liabilities.

Net worth alone does not entirely encompass one's financial health. We must dig deeper. We have to take a closer examination of one's age compared to their net worth and income to obtain a truer assessment of financial health.

For example, a 25-year-old making $45,000 a year, with a $90,000 net worth, is in much better financial health than a 60-year-old making $250,000, with a $200,000 net worth.

The 60-year has a much larger income and net worth than the 25-year-old, so how could it be that the 25-year-old is in better financial health? The answer is two-fold.

The 25-year-old has a higher income-to-net worth ratio and, more importantly, she has many more years to earn an income and thus, more time to increase their net worth than the 60-year-old does.

The process of increasing one's net worth is also two-fold.

First, it involves raising one's assets and simultaneously reducing one's liabilities. As you contribute to a retirement plan on your job or save in a CD or money market account, you are increasing your assets.

Conversely, as you pay down your mortgage, auto loans, or credit card debt, you are reducing liabilities. These two actions, in combination with one another, are a powerful way to increase your net worth quickly and thus, achieve financial dignity.

Back to our 60-year-old. She may only have 5 or 6 years until retirement, meaning she will only be able to save and invest for another few years. At retirement, it is also highly likely she will begin to reduce her assets because she is now in spend-down mode, meaning she is withdrawing from her investment and savings accounts to keep her lifestyle in retirement.

This action can reduce her net worth. Remember, net worth is calculated by subtracting liabilities from assets. If you now have fewer assets than what you had the previous year, your net worth will probably be lower than what it was the previous year.

Coveting what others have or trying to "Keep up with the Joneses" is counterproductive at any stage of life. This destructive behavior is most damaging in the months and years leading up to and in retirement. The reason for this is simple.

In retirement, many of us are on a steady or fixed income. We no longer have the luxury of time to make up any excesses for bad spending habits and unwise purchases.

With recent medical advances, we are now living longer than we ever have and so much so that longevity is a risk factor as it relates to our financial health. With longevity as a risk factor, our retirement nest egg will only last so long. This is true for those with reasonable and sound budgets and for those with no budget.

If you add profligate, reckless spending into the mix, this can lead to a nightmare retirement scenario where one runs out of money before they run out of time.

This reckless behavior is no respecter of person. Those from every walk of life can fall prey to this insidious spending trap. Blue-collar workers, white-collar workers, business owners, 9 to 5 employees—all are vulnerable.

No one is immune and ALL are susceptible, so we must be aware of this unhealthy tendency and root it out sooner, rather than later.

I am convinced that unnecessary, excess spending, in and of itself, does not and cannot make us happy. On the contrary, it only leads to long-term unhappiness, undue stress, and financial ruin.

Renowned gerontologist Karl Pillermer of Cornell University authored a book entitled "30 Lessons for Living: Tried and True Advice." In this insightful and thought-provoking book, he asks over 1,000 Americans over the age of 65 to share key lessons they have learned on living, loving, and finding happiness. Some of what the author found from the interviewees surprised him. Most of what he found was unsurprising.

None of these wise senior citizens said you should choose your work based on how much money you want to make.

None of them said that to be happy, you should try to work harder just to buy more stuff.

Interestingly, not one of them said you should gauge your success based upon the perceived success of those around you.

What they did say, however, is the things that money cannot buy, like true friendships and spending quality time with family, are much more valuable than accumulating more stuff.

I think those are wise words to live by.

HOW WE COVET

I think we begin to covet at a very early age when our minds are still developing and are very impressionable. This is an emotional response that is triggered when we see something we like. A shiny new object, for instance. Or maybe we see something that appears to bring happiness or joy to someone else.

We want that same joy.

We, too, want to be happy and we figure, "If it makes them happy, then it will probably make me happy too. So, I want whatever it is they have!"

In the psychological thriller "The Silence of the Lambs," there is a very memorable line by Sir Anthony Hopkins's character, Dr. Hannibal Lecter. He is schooling a young and ambitious FBI recruit, Clarice Starling, played by Jodi Foster, in her quest to find a serial killer on the loose.

Dr. Lecter says to Clarice, "We begin by coveting what we see every day...and don't your eyes move over the things you want?"

This bit of sage advice by the brilliant, but criminally insane serial killer himself, proved to be very instrumental in helping young Agent Starling find the killer.

As a psychiatrist, Dr. Lecter understood full well the power and effect of those who covet or want what others have and his character understood that unhealthy desire could potentially lead one to do terrible things. As in the case of "Buffalo Bill," it could even lead someone to commit murder.

Even in real life, we see evidence of people doing wild and crazy things due to coveting what others have. This would include beauty, fame, fortune, success, and perceived happiness.

All these things, of course, are in the eye of the beholder.

The famous movie star or athlete could very well be in an unhealthy relationship.

The successful businessman could be carrying so much debt that he is one bad deal away from financial ruin.

For this book, I am using the words covet, jealousy, and envy, interchangeably. What we are talking about here is not simply longing for, or desiring, what others have. We are talking about acting on these emotions. We are talking about changing our everyday habits because of these emotions.

These emotions, in and of themselves, may not be harmful but, when these emotions start to alter our thoughts, our actions, and most importantly, our behavior, they can become toxic and damaging to our psyche and, more importantly, to our finances.

According to some researchers, a form of jealousy is present in infants as early as 5 to 6 months of age. In a study conducted in 2002 [6], an experimental condition was shown to provoke jealousy in 6-and 12-month-old infants by having mothers attend to and affectionately interact with an infant doll.

Infants expressed sadness, anger, and protested their mother's interactions with the doll, and approached the mother repeatedly, showing that they were sensitive to the loss of her attention.

Whether we know it or not, these feelings of jealousy and envy can remain with us through adolescence and into adulthood. It may lurk right below the surface or even be full-blown and in your face.

A 1999 study [7] concluded that "children younger than eight years old are cognitively and psychologically defenseless against advertising." It is estimated that a child in America will see around 20,000 TV commercials a year — 55 per day. Add billboards, magazines, and the

Internet, and the figure rises to 3,000 advertisements a day.

Why is that?

Children have long been seen as a target for advertisers. In 1983, companies spent $100 million advertising to children. By 2009, that figure had risen to $17 billion.

Those of us who have children know that these advertisements have a huge influence over them and are responsible for us spending around $150 billion a year. Think about it.

Parents facing a toy store tantrum may be willing to buy the product to get the kid to stop screaming. If left unchecked, this behavior can linger for many years.

Advertisers and marketing executives understand full well how what we see influences our thoughts and our behavior. This effect is especially pronounced when the influencer is someone we can relate to, or even more potent, someone we admire.

Teenage boys in high school look up to the athletes, the jocks.

"The jocks have all the girls, so I want to be like them," the non-jocks say.

Teenage girls look up to the cheerleaders, the pretty girls.

"The pretty girls never have a problem getting dates. They are popular, so I want to be like them."

Adults are certainly not immune from this tendency to emulate those they think have it all together, either.

Men look up to other men who live in nicer homes.

The ones who drive nice cars.

Who send their kids to private schools and take their families on fabulous vacations.

"Those guys are living their best life, so I want to be like them," the other men say.

Women look up to other women they see in movies and magazines—those with air-brushed photos and tiny waists.

"They are glamorous, so I want to be like them," they say.

What does this all look like put into action?

"If the captain of the football team is wearing a polo shirt, I want it as well."

"If Susie Q, the lead cheerleader, wears her hair a certain way, I must change my hairstyle."

"If Bob moves to Gated Hills, I need to move there as well."

"If 'Fabulousa' is wearing Vera Wang at the Oscars, it must be time for some new Sequins."

The thing to keep in mind here is that these individuals are making a conscious, or more likely, an unconscious decision to go out and spend money on stuff that they ordinarily would NOT be spending money on.

This is money they may need for other, more pressing needs but, unfortunately, those things will just have to wait.

I remember going to pick up rent from a former tenant for a property I owned. There was a big screen TV in the living room I had not seen before.

I commented, "That is a nice TV you have there."

She replied, "Yes, it is, thanks. I am having some friends over this weekend, so of course, I just had to get it."

First, let's be honest. She did not have to get the TV.

Secondly, a cursory look around the home would show that those funds may have been put to better use. Now, I know how this may sound. This is not a value judgment on her, but a statement of fact.

When she completed the rental application, a credit check was performed, so I had a fairly good idea about her finances. Here again, remember the phrase, "We buy things we don't need with money we don't have to impress people we may not even like."

I don't know how she felt about the guests she planned to entertain, but I am quite certain that, if the invitees genuinely cared about her wellbeing, it would not have mattered to them what size TV she had.

It would be the laughs, the fun, and the fellowship of friends that mattered to them the most.

THE PAST SHAPES THE PRESENT

I believe that the key to financial wellness and dignity is to first come to terms with and fully understand your belief system about money. It is exceedingly difficult, if not impossible, to achieve financial dignity until you first develop a mindset that cultivates and nurtures an environment that is conducive to financial health.

In our early formative years, we hear and see things that are stored in our subconscious for later use. As a small child, you may not even understand what money is or what it does, but you do sense that, when those closest to you are yelling at each other, something is wrong.

You do understand that those are negative emotions and, when you are finally old enough to understand the concept of money, you retrieve those memories.

You remember those toxic arguments your parents may have had and associate those arguments with finances – good or bad.

Those memories, whether good or bad, become the basis for how you see the role of money and finances in your life today.

With that in mind, there are a few questions you need to ask yourself during this critical self-discovery process.

Did those closest to you talk about money in a healthy way when you were a child?

Were there arguments about money?

Were there times when your family went without because of a lack of funds?

Did your family seem to have it all?

Was there an abundance?

Did you have a spendthrift parent – always buying more stuff?

Did that never-ending spending lead to even more arguments?

Understand that the answers to these questions shaped your thoughts about money today, whether you are consciously aware of it or not.

After answering those questions, we need to understand the true purpose of financial resources in our lives.

"Are my financial resources designed to enhance my life, allowing me to spend time with those I most care about? Or are those resources simply meant for me to continue buying more stuff?"

A $100,000 Bentley will perform the same task as a $25,000 Hyundai, which is to get you from point A to point B as efficiently as possible. Likewise, a seven-bedroom, five-bathroom mini-mansion will supply the same basic purpose as a three-bedroom, two-bath house, which is to supply shelter from the elements.

The previous story of our nice family from the woods was taught this concept. Sure, the Bentley and the mini-mansion have some bells and whistles that their entry-level counterparts do not but, at the end of the day, they will all supply the same base functions. The entry-level versions will supply those functions at a price point the average person can afford.

I have a client who is what I like to call an "Extreme Saver."

She is saving and investing upwards of 60% of her take-home pay, which is far higher than the rate the average American is saving.

Her home and car are both paid for.

She only buys the necessities and even then, the necessities must be on sale.

She rarely takes a vacation.

She uses coupons.

She drives her car until the wheels fall off and, when she is forced to replace it, she buys a practical, used car that is well within her budget.

As a result of this disciplined, and some may say, constrained lifestyle, she has amassed a large portfolio compared to her income.

At one of our semi-annual meetings, I congratulated her on building such a nice retirement nest egg, asking her how she came to be such an aggressive saver.

She said her family did not have a lot growing up.

She said sometimes there was more month than money in the household and wanted to make sure that she was never in such a crisis as an adult.

A lack of resources caused her family to struggle at times, leaving an indelible impression on her.

One she will never forget.

Her early experience with money was not a positive one, and thus, has shaped how she manages her finances today.

Likewise, I had a great-aunt with a similar experience.

She grew up during the great depression. I remember discussing with her why she always wanted to have access to at least $1,000. Keep in mind that $1,000 was considered a healthy cash reserve for many folks during that era and especially for those with very modest incomes like my great-aunt.

Like my client, she too remembered the desperate times and never wanted to see them again. Neither of them ever wanted to be "*broke*" and they never were!

On the other end of the spectrum are those who grew up in a family with no financial worries.

Their parents may have even been philanthropic and donated to their favorite charities.

For them, summer is a verb more than a noun.

They have vacation homes - plural.

Only the best will do. The youngsters in the household saw and became accustomed to that lifestyle. As an adult, that experience may have caused them to spend like there is no tomorrow.

Regardless of whether their current financial resources are like their parents or not, these folks never experienced financial anxieties. For them, things always seemed to just work themselves out.

Now, as adults, they have to deal with an economic reality that may not justify the extravagant lifestyle they feel entitled to.

Left unchecked, these repressed memories can lead to *pathos*. According to Merriam-Webster: The Greek word *pathos* means "suffering," "experience," or "emotion." It was borrowed into English in the 16th century, and for English speakers, the term usually refers to the emotions produced by tragedy or a depiction of tragedy. *Pathos* has quite a few kin in English. *Pathetic* is used to describe things that move us to pity.

Let's not let our memories as children make us pathetic as adults.

TAKE ACTION!

By this point, you now have a better understanding of how your past experiences around money have shaped your thoughts, actions, and financial behavior today.

So, what do you do now?

First things first—get a plan of action. That plan should be written and developed with the advice and counsel of a trusted guide or financial coach. This guide should be knowledgeable in finance and has spent time getting to know your dreams, goals, and financial resources. Together, you need to prioritize the things that are most important to you and your family. That might include getting out of debt, saving for a child's or grandchild's future college expenses, building an adequate cash reserve, or making sure that you can retire in the lifestyle you envision for yourself.

Second, develop a budget. A budget, in its simplest terms, is just knowing how much money is coming into your home; versus how much is leaving. This is Cash Flow 101.'

There are too many individuals, organizations, and even the Federal Government who either do not budget adequately or have no budget at all. As we have discussed ad nauseam, when we don't budget, we tend to spend more than we make.

We live above our means.

We have more month than money.

We experience a cash-flow shortage.

Call it what you want, but not having a budget is a recipe for financial ruin. Maybe not today or tomorrow, but in the future.

There are many types and ways to budget. There is the old-school 'envelope method.' Folks back in the day would put a certain amount of cash in various envelopes. The amount put in each envelope would be based on how much they plan to spend on that expenditure. If they spent more than what was planned for, they would take cash from another envelope. This method is truly old-school and may not be practical today.

There are countless spreadsheets, online budgets, and budget apps out there for us to use.

I've seen people come into my office with their income and expenses hand-written on a single sheet of paper.

What is the best type of budget? The answer to that question is the same as the question of, "What is the best diet plan out there?" It's the one you are willing to stick with.

If the envelope method works for you, do it.

If you are someone who likes logging onto the computer to watch your budget daily, more power to you. Some folks like the convenience and flexibility of having an app on their smartphone. It doesn't matter. Just pick one and stick with it!

Third, having an adequate cash reserve is a close second to developing a budget. A cash reserve is sometimes referred to as a "rainy-day fund."

What if the car breaks down or the roof caves in? We don't want to have to take out loans or tap into credit cards. We need readily available cash.

It's best to plan for three to six months of your regularly occurring expenses in a cash account. As an example, if your monthly expenses total $3,000, you should have between $9,000 and $18,000 saved.

Why three to six months? If you get sick or hurt and can't work, you will need a few months of cash to float you until your disability income policy kicks in. This assumes, of course, you have a disability income policy. Also, if you are laid off, which we all know can happen, it could take a few months to secure practical employment. An adequate cash reserve can mean the difference between staying in your home or eviction.

As discussed earlier, most Americans do not have anywhere near three months, let alone six months of their regular expenses saved. If that's you, you need to save to reach that amount systematically.

You could set up an automatic debit from your paycheck or even your checking account to go to a savings or money market account.

You could check with a financial firm to invest monthly in one of their guaranteed certificates.

The destination account should be separate from the origination account. It also needs to draw some interest and be liquid and accessible in case of an emergency. That's the whole idea, right?

Maybe you talk to your payroll department about having $50 per pay period go to your credit union account or direct your bank to move $100 each month from your checking account to a new savings account. Whatever the amount, it needs to be automatic. This will help ensure you stay on track.

At some point, we will all need to spend money on something or another. Before making that purchase, though, ask yourself honestly if it is a need or want.

If it is indeed a need, can it be bought someplace else cheaper?

If it is just a want, ask yourself if this purchase will enhance your life in some form or fashion.

Far too many times, purchases are made simply on impulse. Maybe it is "on sale" or you are in line to buy other items and look over and see something you feel you just have to have at that moment.

Many will find that these impulse purchases are rarely wants, let alone needs. After making impulse purchases, some people receive a release of endorphins. Endorphins are a hormone that can be produced after an experience that makes us feel good. Think of eating chocolate, finishing a good run, or being intimate with your partner.

According to Wikipedia, the euphoria one can experience from endorphins being released is like that produced by opioids! Yes indeed!

Some people are addicted to shopping and it's no wonder that retail is a multi-billion-dollar-a-year industry. Shopping makes some of us feel good.

To help overcome the potential emotional effects of making a purchase, wait a day or two to see if you still want the item. If you still want that item, try to find it someplace else on sale.

Use cash for nonessential items instead of credit cards. People tend to spend more when using credit cards instead of cash. Psychologically, using cash seems to be a bit more painful than using a credit card, where you won't see the financial damage for weeks.

You also want to work with your financial coach on investing for the future. These investments need to be tied to a goal you have set up for yourself. Before investing, some questions need to be answered.

As an example, if you plan to retire in 10 years, how much is required for you and your family to retire in the lifestyle you envision?

Are you eligible to contribute to a company retirement plan?

Are matching employer contributions available?

How much do you need to contribute to receive the full matching contributions?

Are you eligible to contribute to a Roth IRA?

Does it make sense for you to contribute to a Roth IRA?

How much should you be contributing each pay period or each month to cover any shortfalls for retirement?

A competent financial advisor should be well equipped to help you answer those and other financial questions you might have.

Now you better understand that excess or thrifty spending both begins and ends in the mind.

You realize we first have to reframe our thinking around how to best use our hard-earned dollars.

You have created a budget you plan to stick with.

You have set up or are saving an adequate cash reserve.

You are contributing a suitable amount to a retirement plan.

You may now find that you have neither the wherewithal nor, much more importantly, the desire to keep up with the Joneses.

You also may find that you are too busy minding your own financial business to care about what John and Jane Doe are doing with theirs.

That, my friends, is the goal.

ENDNOTES

1. The Psychology of Money by Morgan Housel

2. Will Rogers, The Total Money Makeover: A Proven Plan for Financial Fitness

3. CNBC article, "INVEST IN YOU: READY. SET. GROW," published Wed, Jul 28, 2021

4. Business Insider article Personal Finance, "Rich and Famous Celebrities Who Lost All Their Money" published Aug 8, 2019

5. Love Money article, "Lottery winners who won millions but ended up with nothing" published Nov 30, 2021

6. Evidence of Jealousy in Young Infants · by SL Hart · 2016

7. Report of the APA Task Force on Advertising and Children Feb 2004

CPSIA information can be obtained
at www.ICGtesting.com
Printed in the USA
LVHW081651080223
739012LV00004B/911